Instructions for using AR

LET AUGMENTED REALITY CHANGE HOW YOU READ A BOOK

With your smartphone, iPad or tablet you can use the **Neighbur Vue** app to invoke the augmented reality experience to literally read outside the book.

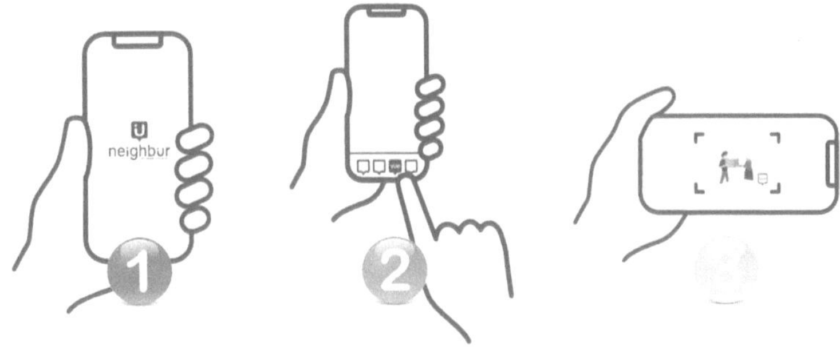

1. Notice the spelling: download the **Neighbur Vue app** from the **Apple App Store** or **Google Play**
2. Open and select the vue (vue) option
3. Point your lens at the full image with the vue and enjoy the augmented reality experience.

Go ahead and try it right now with this image.

Once the content begins, click the '**Lock**' icon to lock the content onto your phone.

Praise for **Free and Rich Beyond Wealthy**

*"**Free and Rich Beyond Wealthy** by Gisele Maxwell is the perfect guide for anyone interested in starting and building their own business. Starting your own business is no small task, but Gisele takes you through the journey of doing it with the right mindset, passion, and the personal growth you never thought was possible! I am convinced that you can save yourself a lot of time, money and struggle while achieving your greatness when you follow the path in **Free and Rich Beyond Wealthy**!"*

– **Mary Vivian Braunschneider**
Executive Coach and Certified Consultant
for Proctor Gallagher Institute

"I am convinced that most of us women want to have our own business so that we can have time, money and freedom. However, we are scared of taking the risk, often due to lack of knowledge about where to start and how to proceed. I wish I had this book to help me decide whether to continue my law career or start my own coaching business. I wanted to be free and rich, and Gisele explains exactly how to do that, without having to go through the emotional overwhelm. This book is especially valuable at this time, since a lot of us will be reinventing ourselves personally and professionally!"

– **Katia Stern**
Author of *You Were Born WOW*

*"Gisele Maxwell's book is a great refresher for any businessperson and entrepreneur. She combines powerful nuances of mindset and building a business with ease. Precise practices coupled with great business ethics, **Free and Rich Beyond Wealthy** is a MUST read!"*

– **Judy O'Beirn**
Best-Selling Author of *Unwavering Strength* Series,
President, Hasmark Publishing International

"Gisele's abundant experience in the corporate sector is prevalent in her new book, ***Free and Rich Beyond Wealthy****. She offers her readers useful tips towards creating sustainable business practices. This book hones in on mindset and values, and is definitely a great roadmap towards starting a new business."*

– **Pashmina P.**
International Best-Selling Author of *The Cappuccino Chronicles* Trilogy,
Marketing Director, Hasmark Publishing International

*"****Free and Rich Beyond Wealthy*** *is a must-read for anyone who is ready to live life on their terms and pursue their true life's passion. Gisele will not only cause you to dream big, but will also share amazing and practical insight on how to build your business and create a clear path to your success."*

– **Darryl Bell**
Founder and CEO of Hope and Exchange,
Author of *We Are Creators*

FREE *and* RICH

Beyond Wealthy

GISELE MAXWELL

Published by
Hasmark Publishing
www.hasmarkpublishing.com

First Edition

Disclaimer

This book is designed to provide information and motivation to our readers. It is sold with the understanding that the publisher is not engaged to render any type of psychological, legal, or any other kind of professional advice. The content of each article is the sole expression and opinion of its author, and not necessarily that of the publisher. No warranties or guarantees are expressed or implied by the publisher's choice to include any of the content in this volume. Neither the publisher nor the individual author(s) shall be liable for any physical, psychological, emotional, financial, or commercial damages, including, but not limited to, special, incidental, consequential or other damages. Our views and rights are the same: You are responsible for your own choices, actions, and results.

Editor: Allison Burney
allison.burney@gmail.com

Cover & Book Design: Anne Karklins
anne@hasmarkpublishing.com

ISBN 13: 978-1-989756-23-2
ISBN 10: 1989756239

To my family

"*Those who live are those who fight.*"
– Victor Hugo

TABLE OF CONTENTS

ACKNOWLEDGEMENTS

As I start to write my acknowledgements, I can't help reflecting back on the journey that prompted me to write this book. Never in my wildest dreams would I have thought of writing a book on how to become free by starting your own business when I was a successful scientist, or even after I became an entrepreneur. This book, to me, is really a testimony that every event in your life has an outcome, and that the way you respond to it ends up creating your path. I am grateful for all the events in my life, the good ones and the not so good ones, that have led to the writing of this book. Many people have influenced me, and since it might not be proper to name the "bad" influences (or at least the ones who were not very pleasant to deal with at certain times), I do want to thank them for their contribution. Our strength lies in our ability to take any kind of criticism and build from it.

The first person I want to thank is Mary Vivian Braunschneider, who started it all for me when she called me out of the blue about a year ago. Mary is a wonderful and generous person who became my mentor and helped me shed a different light on my career, and then became my friend. She is now part of my journey, as we are building a series of podcasts together to help people reinvent themselves and become entrepreneurs.

Another wonderful mentor that I would like to thank is Peggy McColl. She is a true inspiration and our one-on-one sessions have been key in motivating me to pursue writing a book.

I would also like to acknowledge the invaluable support of Hasmark Publishing International. Judy O'Beirn's team is amazing. Their skills, dedication, and willingness to work with authors to help them accomplish their dreams have been instrumental throughout this journey.

The amazing photographs throughout this book were taken by a very talented young artist, Cesar Molina (@Nerdgangceas)ing, and I thank him for making this even more unique.

The beautiful cover picture was taken by my life partner, William Mascote, and I am really happy that he was inspired to take such a beautiful shot that day. Thank you for standing by my side always.

The character "Balty" that is following your journey in this book was created and drawn by my niece, Gabriela Lizama. I am deeply grateful for her wonderful talent and her beautiful personality.

My family has been nothing but supportive of me for as long as I can remember, and once again, they have cheered on and congratulated me with all their hearts every step of the way on this journey. I thank my Mom who was always keen on reading every single chapter of the book as soon as it was written. I really appreciated her valuable comments and edits. I love you all more than words can ever describe.

INTRODUCTION

Awaken the business beast in you

The Rev. Martin Luther King Jr. once said, "I have a dream," and from there proceeded to change the world and make it a better place. We all have a dream; we all have a song in us that is worth singing to the world. We can all achieve greatness. It takes work and dedication, but most things do, and the journey and rewards far exceed the investment. This book shows you how to build your own business to achieve your dreams of greatness and freedom. I write from my own experience and hope that you can learn from my mistakes, too, and obtain a blueprint of an easier path to success as an entrepreneur.

Bruce Lee said, "Your state of mind is everything." Why would anyone start their own business? It doesn't matter if you are fresh out of school, working for a corporation, big or small, or maybe even retired. One trait is common to all entrepreneurs: they all have a dream of achieving something bigger and making the world a better place. For some of us, it is about fulfilling a passion and helping people in the process; for others, it is about a vision of something that will make people's lives better, even if they are not aware of it yet. Steve Jobs built Apple from his vision that he could "make a contribution to the world by making tools for the mind that advance humankind." Bill Gates had a passion for computers, too, and decided that he would put one on every home and office desk to better people's lives. You don't have to be Steve Jobs or Bill Gates to build your business, but you do need to have a vision and a passion. Whether your plan is to build the next Google or to open a flower shop, you need the same mindset. Real success is measured by how much you grow and who you become as you build your business. Money is a byproduct, not a motivator. Following your purpose is key.

They say timing is everything, and it's certainly crucial when you decide to become an entrepreneur. It's all about being ready. This is how it happened to me.

About 15 years ago, I was a successful corporate scientist. With a Ph.D. in physics from my native France and advanced study at Stanford University, my idea of a good career was to work as a scientist for a "stable" company. Because I am really good, both as a scientist and as a manager, I was very successful and kept being promoted. But I quickly learned that my success depended on the company's, so my job was far from stable. After a few years with the same company, in which I had become a prominent figure, I was told that the company might relocate abroad.

That scared me, of course. And because my then-husband worked for the same company, it would be double jeopardy for us if we both lost our jobs. So, I left to work for another company that I thought was more stable. It was a more early-stage company, but its fine technology promised big successes. The company had been courting me for almost two years. A month after I was hired to work on a key project, I was informed that the company was hurting and to reduce its work force, the group I was a part of would be cut. Fortunately, I found a way to generate quick, substantial revenue from the technology I was hired to work on, so I was able to stay as well as to save half of my group. But the experience did not leave me with a feeling of security or stability. So, when an investor friend talked to me about starting my own business and being able to work on whatever I wanted as both scientist and chief executive officer (CEO), I was ready and jumped at the opportunity. I was in the right state of mind to start my own business and my reward was not just success and recognition but also tremendous personal growth. After all, it is about who you become in the process.

So what stops so many people? There is a reason many of our excellent business ideas never see the light.

"The fears we don't face become our limits," says Robin Sharma. Sometimes we are not even aware of our own fears, so we can't address what we don't know. We don't realize that our beliefs have become fears that block us from success. They are fatal for a new business. So how do you address your fears?

The first step is to acknowledge the nagging inner voice that tells you that your idea is crazy, that you are not an expert, and it won't work. Recognizing that voice is like entertaining an idea—offer it some cake, but DO NOT IGNORE IT. Ignoring your feelings and fears will not make them go away; it will amplify them. Replace the statement "this will not work" with "how can I make this work?" Be prepared for the fact that many people will tell you that you are crazy and will remind you that there are more "stable" jobs in corporations. They don't say it to be mean, but their belief system is different from yours. Their opinions need to be recognized, too.

Your nagging inner voice may accompany you for the whole journey of entrepreneurship, going so far as to tell you that you are not cut out to be a business owner, let alone a CEO. This is called the Imposter Syndrome. I know it well, occasionally having suffered from it during my 12 years as a CEO. Fortunately, I belonged to a group of good people with the same problem, and we helped each other through it. Having that kind of group and sharing experiences with like-minded people is critical to growing your own business.

My online program, "Free and Rich Beyond Wealthy," can help you create a whole community of business owners who are ready to share, help and brainstorm with you. Along the way, you will encounter so many "well-intentioned" detractors that a group of people who support you, instead, will help you "live" your purpose.

People often think you need education, experience and/or money to start a business. Countless success stories prove that this is far from the truth. Andrew Carnegie, who was once one of the richest businessmen anywhere, had very little formal education and instead learned by reading. The highly successful company Earthbound Farms was started by a couple on their 2.5-acre farm. Its growth stemmed from their desire to provide food grown in harmony with nature. It quickly became the brand that offered the easiest access to organic foods. What was most important to the company's success was that the couple had a purpose and were living it.

Why is having a purpose so important? Because if you want to grow rich beyond being merely wealthy, your purpose must be more than just making money, though money can be part of it. Purpose drives passion and vice versa, and advancing personal growth while starting your business will ensure success. Again, it is about who you become in the process. A fulfilled life is the ultimate reward of the journey.

When I started and then grew my company, I made good money—one of the rewards—but I gained recognition, respect and a stellar reputation in the scientific community. I got to write for prestigious journals and I became a keynote speaker, addressing thousands of people in beautiful places. While money comes and goes, these other perks don't fade away. I could also set my own schedule almost every day. Freedom, growth and riches become within your reach when you start your own business and grow it.

"But how can I do that when I don't know where to start?" The fact that you are reading this book means you already know the answer. As you continue reading, you will be given a set of essential tools. I have gathered all the knowledge I have acquired as a business owner, and I am sharing it with you to accelerate an otherwise tricky process if you were left to learn these things on your own. I explain in full detail every step of the process, from assessing your idea to growing your business and perhaps even going global. But my work will only pay off for you as a new entrepreneur if you use the tools.

Reading this book means that you are committed to your new venture, but then you need to take responsibility and action. The online program (www.freeandrichbeyondwealthy.com) linked to this book includes a list of resources that make it easier for you to accomplish certain tasks. You also have access to a biweekly Q&A session with me. But it is completely your responsibility to embark on your beautiful adventure.

Get started and *then* feel the passion, not the other way around. Too many people wait to "find" their passion. While you can find many things—a car, a house, a partner or a pet—passion is not one of them. It would be like trying to "find" sadness. Passion comes from being energized by what you do. You feel that energy particularly when you are good at what you do. But, purely as a feeling, passion comes and goes. There will be days when you wake up feeling excited and ready to take on the world, and there will be days when you will be paralyzed by fear, wondering why you ever decided to go on such a roller coaster. The good news is: fear is a sign of growth. You will feel fear once in a while, but you will learn that comfort is your enemy. *Feel the Fear and Do It Anyway*, Susan Jeffers' excellent book, can help with the feelings of the particular kind of hopelessness that can arise in entrepreneurs.

The only way to remove fear is to act. Fear is mostly in the unknown. Once you go into action, every step you take removes a little bit of the unknown and, therefore, the fear. Since you have made the decision to become an entrepreneur and enjoy all of the beautiful rewards that come with it, all you need to do is keep moving through the negative feelings that will show up on the way.

We learn from our mistakes (I made many as an entrepreneur), we grow from rejection, we don't give up and we move forward. Success is at the end of the road!

So, let's build a business!

CHAPTER 1

Do you think you have a brilliant idea?

One Monday morning, when I was a program manager of a top-priority scientific development at a successful Silicon Valley start-up—and going with the ups and downs of the early stages—I got a call from a friend who had founded two successful companies fresh out of her Ph.D. "Will you have breakfast with me tomorrow to discuss an idea that might be great for both of our careers?" she asked intriguingly. When I met her, she said that she wanted to start a company with me—that she had the funds but she wanted me to supply the ideas. I told her that I needed to think about it. I was a happy scientist and manager supporting other people's visions, and the thought of starting my own business—and making my own visions happen—had never crossed my mind. The concept that I could also work for my own vision and make it happen was completely foreign to me. The morning she made the proposal, I was at a loss for ideas—but ready to try something new.

Earl Nightingale said, "Everything begins with an idea." In 2004, Matt Maloney and Mike Evans were hard at work and tired

of calling restaurants for good take-out food. That led to their idea to start a one-stop shop for food delivery. That became GrubHub. They fixed a problem with a simple solution and made the lives of many other people easier as a result. GrubHub went public and is now valued at around $3 billion. This is the key: a brilliant idea needs to solve a widespread problem. If your business only serves you, most likely it will fail. Similarly, an idea solely based on a cool but somewhat useless technology is unlikely to go anywhere. Then what about Steve Jobs and Apple? They invented and marketed things that people didn't need at the time—but they had a vision. They wanted to make tools to advance mankind, and they built their business on that vision. It was not just a cool idea; it was about serving mankind.

That's the point. To assess the value of your idea, you need to answer these questions: What problem needs solving? Does it affect other people? Will my solution benefit everybody? Again, making money is a byproduct of serving people. After you have determined that your idea will indeed make people's lives better, there will be more questions to ask to evaluate the market you want to enter.

You need to figure out if you are going to be a small fish in a big pond or a big fish in a small pond. If the market is huge, then only a small fraction of it will secure a profitable business. If you are addressing a niche market, you need to capture a larger share of it. Of course, nothing should prevent you from becoming a big fish in a big pond! Taking stock of a market entails asking new questions. It is essential to learn market size, market trends, demographics and geography. You also need to determine whether people are willing to purchase your product or service, and at what price. Asking friends and family and associates is valuable, but another, more advanced way is to take a survey. Several companies will help you devise a survey and send it to a panel of people. Their rates are not prohibitive, and answers from a sample of 200 or more people provide invaluable data. SurveyMonkey and PeopleFish offer the service, and there are others you can find online. You need to come up with a profile of your target audience. You will need to ask specific questions: Who are my customers? How old are they? Where do they live? How much money do they earn? Is my market gender specific, for instance, women's clothes? Your answers will show you your target audience.

Once the market size is assessed and your potential customers are identified, you need to know your competition. Who are my competitors? How well are they doing? What do people like or dislike about them? How am I unique? What differentiator do I offer? Surveys can help with some of these questions, too. For example, if you decide to start a flower business, ask yourself what it is that will make people buy flowers from you rather than at a supermarket where they do their other shopping? The answer may be that your flowers look better or that you provide your customers with a different experience. They feel good when they buy your flowers. What distinguishes you from your competitors is what gives you power.

It's also important to understand your industry. In addition to reading about it and talking to people in the industry, you can attend trade shows. In the flower business, you could learn about the different types of plants or flowers so you could specialize in a few varieties, such as orchids, tropical plants or bonsai. Knowing your industry tells you where you fit in it, what you bring that is unique and how the industry supply chain works. Where do you obtain the seeds or plants? Do you need a home delivery system? Can you work with other flower shops to provide an enhanced customer experience? A dialogue like that is what prompted the creation of FTD. Florists' Telegraph Delivery was founded in 1910 to help customers send flowers remotely and on the same day by using florists in the FTD network nearer the recipient. This shows how providing a particular kind of service can become a huge success.

Finally, you need to study carefully whether your product is sensitive to market trends. If you are in the clothing business, for example, you will have to attend or follow fashion shows.

The trends in other businesses, such as food and the automotive markets, may be subtler to discern, or trends that are more global, such as "going green." Whatever the case, understanding trends is key to being able to adjust quickly.

Once you have done this primary market research, you can investigate other kinds of market research by reading market reports and going to meetings of business organizations such as chambers of commerce and economic development centers.

You can also speak directly with people who fit your customer profile. For example, go to a flower shop and ask customers what they want from the experience of buying flowers, how they rate their experience with this particular shop and what could have been done to improve that experience. The secret to success is to ask and keep asking. At trade shows, ask people in a particular industry how it works and who the suppliers are, and then talk to the suppliers. Learn from people who have engaged in the industry and are still active it. There is no need to reinvent everything.

After you have gathered the information about your industry and your market, you are in a good position to differentiate your product or service and make your business unique and unlike what already exists. The CarMax story provides a perfect example of finding a great differentiator. In the early 1990s, at a time when Circuit City was a chain of retail stores, two executives interviewed people about their experiences buying used cars. Everyone had a dreadful story to tell. Buying a car from a dealership, especially a used one, was an ordeal no one looked forward to. With what they learned, Richard Sharp (CEO) and Austin Ligon (VP) decided to shift the consumer paradigm to provide customers with a pleasant experience. They removed one of the components of the car buying experience, price negotiation, and changed it to a "no-haggle" price concept. They added a money-back guarantee and introduced high standards of inspection and other requirements for the cars. They also provided big car lots and huge inventories to choose from. CarMax did not become profitable immediately, but it is now a

Fortune 500 company that has prompted other car dealerships to follow their lead. What most distinguished CarMax, of course, was the "no-haggle" policy. Prices were kept low and fixed.

Your market assessment will help you determine the pricing of your product or service. If you conduct a survey, a simple question such as, "How much would you be willing to pay for such a product/service?" will indicate what you can expect. What matters is not what you think your product or service is worth, but how much your customers are willing to pay for it. I have often heard people say, "I am going to sell my house for at least this much because my neighbors sold theirs for that price." Well, that may give you a ballpark figure, but you won't know the actual value of your house until you sell it! Data about potential customers can also help you identify the best location for your business, what quality customers are looking for and how they would like you to upgrade the convenience of your service. The best proof of success is returning satisfied customers.

Starting a business entails risk-taking and is not for the faint of heart. But if you are aware of the challenges and prepared to meet them, you can lessen the risk. Don't give up until you get the information you need despite occasional setbacks and some "no" responses to your questions. Make a fair assessment of your market; overpromising and underdelivering are among the biggest potential mistakes. Making these preparations should be taken as seriously as an athlete would prepare for the Olympics. Your success depends on a complete understanding of the parameters pertaining to your particular business venture.

Resources:
An inspiring story by an entrepreneur:
Jack Canfield's *Chicken Soup for the Entrepreneur's Soul*
Customer assessment surveys:
SurveyMonkey (http://www.surveymonkey.com) or PeopleFish (https://people.fish/)
Information about trade shows:
Trade Show Advisor (www.trade-show-advisor.com)
Help starting a business:
Free and Rich Beyond Wealthy online course (www.freeandrichbeyondwealthy.com)

CHAPTER 2

The tools you will need and where to find them

"Don't worry, I will help you. I have done it before, and I will pave the road for you." That's what my friend said as she convinced me to start my own business. The assurance was welcome because I had no experience in starting a business. Previously, I only had to focus on my own project and the people reporting to me. Being on my own, making decisions about a business I was creating from the ground up, was the scariest thing I could imagine.

Many tools are needed to start a business. Most often, when I asked for help obtaining a particular one, the problem was my lack of a list of the exact tools I needed. Determining what I needed was a struggle, so this chapter will provide you with the list that I was never given and had to figure out on my own.

"The best investment is in the tools of one's own trade," Benjamin Franklin famously said. This chapter is more technical, but bear in mind that the tools described are efficient only if you use them.

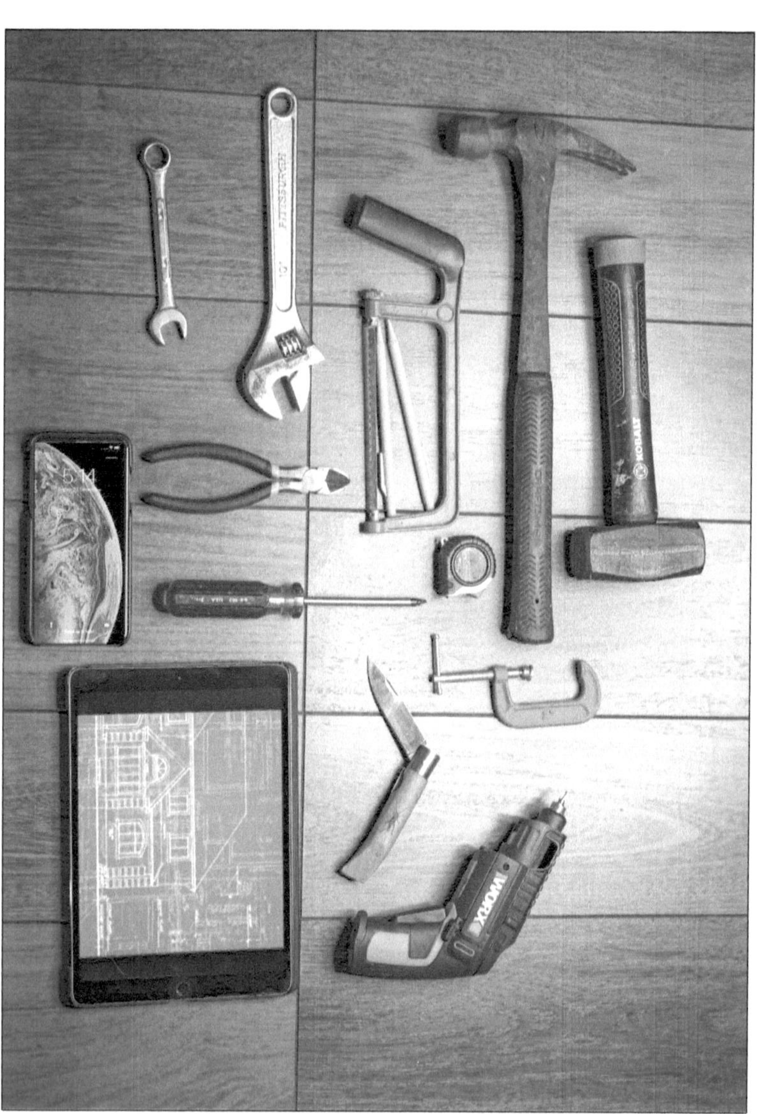
PITTSBURGH
KOBALT
WORX

First, you need a name for your new business. The business name is as important as the title and cover of a book. It will be your customers' first impression of your business. It's all about perception, so the name must reflect your business' purpose—and the feeling you want to elicit when people think about it. A short, to-the-point name is generally better. It should also be easy to pronounce. If your focus is an international market, choose a name people from any culture can say. For example, I chose to name my high-tech company "Shasta Crystals." It was a short name, it related to what we did and where we started, and people everywhere could say it. Keep in mind that, with success, your business name might even become a brand! Brainstorm, make a list of possible names, and then narrow it down to the perfect one.

If you are hesitating between names, you could use social media to conduct a poll. When you have the perfect name, register it with a domain name. I used GoDaddy, which is easy and inexpensive, to secure the name and the domain name for my business and the program linked to this book.

You will also need a business logo. Because it reflects what the business is about, it should be carefully considered. I used Canva software to create my logo, but if you don't want to spend money, there are websites that will do it for free or on a trial basis. After you have determined your preferences, you can get your logo designed and make business cards and letterhead at the same time.

If you are going to present your business idea to banks and investors, or even friends and family, write a document that tells a good, compelling story. You can call it a business plan or a business narrative, but it needs to include the following:

1. **A brief description of your business.** An example: Beautiful Exotic Flowers is about bringing your family joy. Our experience growing and caring for exotic flowers will bring paradise into your home, and we will teach you how to care for your plants.

2. **A clear statement of your vision.** Again, your chance of success is lessened if you don't have a clear vision of the way your business will grow.
3. **A conversation about the opportunity, the markets and the way(s) your business model is unique** (what you are doing better or what problem you are fixing).
4. **Knowledge of your competitors.** How do you assess your competition, and what does that tell you about your business?
5. **A decision about how to sell your product.** Will customers buy from your store, or will you ship it to them? Will they buy from your website? If you are providing a service, do people subscribe as members? Can they pay on a one-time-only basis? Are you selling through other people or websites, such as Amazon or eBay?
6. **A budget or financial forecast.** How much money will you need to build your business? This must be a thorough exercise, which I will discuss at greater length in the next section. But the business plan must include a summary. The forecast will reflect the way(s) you plan to grow your business over the next three to five years. There should also be a summary of the ways you arrived at the numbers.
7. **For fundraising,** a statement of the amount you are seeking, what it is going to be used for and how it will benefit your business, to take it to the next level. I will say more about fundraising later, but even if you are borrowing money from your friends, you must convince them why they should lend to you and what they will get in return. That could be interest, a stake in your business, or some other perk that appeals to them.
8. **A description of your team, including yourself.** Provide details about every person's experience, what their role in the business will be, what unique experience they bring and how well they fit in.

There are online templates for business plans or executive summaries. They are usually free and give you an idea of where to start. Keeping it detailed but simple is a must.

Create a financial spreadsheet to back up your financial forecast. The numbers in the financial forecast must match the ones in the financial spreadsheet. View the financial spreadsheet as a snapshot of your finances when you start and then three to five years into the future. You can customize the spreadsheet, but it should include: your projected revenue, the number of units you plan to sell (if it's a product) and the net profit, which is the difference between the price of your product and the amount it costs to make (or procure, if you are selling retail rather than producing). It must also show a breakdown of your operating expenses. That includes administrative expenses (such as how much accounting costs), sales and marketing (optional at the beginning but as a place-holder for company growth), and operational costs (such as rent, employee payroll and utilities). Finally, there needs to be a line showing headcount and its growth.

A simple template that could be revised looks something like this:

	2020	2021	2022
Revenue ($)			
Units Sold			
Gross Profit ($)			
Operating Expenses			
General and Administrative ($)			
Sales and Marketing ($)			
Operations Costs ($)			
Total Operating Expenses ($)			
Headcount			

The next consideration is location, location, location. The location of your business is among the most important decisions you will make. It will define the tax base, the value of your rent, variations in minimum wage (my company used to be located in San Francisco, where minimum wage was significantly higher than most other places), variations in utility rates and the costs of business licenses and permits.

You must also be aware of the rules in your neighborhood, even if you choose to operate your business out of your home. Some city zoning rules are very strict, especially when potential pollution is involved. In the consulting business I own now, helping some high-tech companies in-house, one of the first questions I am asked is, "Is this a polluting technology? What are the facility requirements?"

Your location could offer some local tax credits, loans or incentives. For example, when I started my business in an underutilized business zone, the Economic Development Center offered an incentive through the Smart Business Center: if we hired employees with no college degree, they would pay their wages for six months. It helped us tremendously at the beginning. We could train people for six months for free!

Another important consideration regarding location (obvious in certain cases and less so in others) is how easy it is to access your business. If your business is retail, look for a location with maximum foot traffic, so people can window shop easily. If you provide an Internet service, the comfort of your home is probably a good first option, which I will explain in Chapter 5.

Then, once you have secured a location, obtain a business license and perhaps apply for a business permit as well. Below is a list of licenses and permits that may be required. Since the location and the nature of your business make a difference, this list gives only a few examples, and may not represent what you need. Then you will have to research it yourself.

1. **Federal and state tax identification number:** most businesses must apply for a federal EIN, or employer identification

number, also known as a tax identification number. This can be done when you incorporate your business. Use this number for tax purposes and if you apply to a line of credit.

2. **General business license:** A general business license to operate in the city in which a business is located is usually required.
3. **Sales tax permit:** If your business sells goods, whether online or offline, and your state requires you to collect sales tax, you may be required to obtain a business permit or a sales tax permit or a seller's permit. Check with your local City Hall or Economic Development Center.
4. **Zoning permit:** Local zoning regulations may limit where certain types of businesses can operate. These regulations apply not only to businesses such as manufacturers and restaurants but also to some home-business owners (neighborhood regulations).
5. **Professional/occupational licenses:** These are regulated by states. If you provide health care or childcare, you may be required to obtain a special professional or occupational license. Other professions, such as law and medicine, are usually regulated and may require special professional licenses.
6. **Environmental permits:** Many state and local governments require certain businesses to obtain special pollution-control permits. For example, if, in the course of your business, you will engage in an activity that entails the discharge of an environmental contaminant into the air or the water, you may have to obtain a special permit. Some cities have very strict environmental regulations.

These are just a few examples. Do the inquiries and research necessary to get the proper licenses and permits to start.

Resources:
Name and Domain name registration: www.GoDaddy.com
Logo: www.canva.com
Business Plan Templates: Microsoft Office Templates
Financial Spreadsheet Templates: Microsoft Office Templates
State and local resources: SBA.gov, City Hall, Economic Development Centers, Chamber of Commerce and others.

CHAPTER 3

Do you value your assets?

I was surprised when my friend Marcus called. We had not spoken in a long time, but, since we had been friends for years, catching up was always enjoyable. When I asked him, "How are you?" his answer was not very cheerful: "I've had better days." He told me that he was in financial trouble because he was not able to pay his tax bill. He said he owed $50,000 for his consulting work for the year and had not seen that liability coming. I could not have been more surprised. Marcus was always very careful, even frugal, with money. When I asked him how bad it was, he said that the IRS was threatening to freeze his accounts and put a lien on his house if he didn't pay the bill. Marcus had collected his consulting fees but had not realized that his tax base as an independent contractor was going to be quite high. As we discussed ways to deal with the existing bill, I asked if he was planning on doing more consulting in the future. His answer was yes, especially when his field, computer science, was in high demand and he could help start many exciting projects. I advised him to incorporate a consulting business so that, in the future, he could avoid the problem.

Why should one incorporate a business? Whether you are a lawyer or selling goods, you should automatically incorporate your business. If you provide consulting services or work as an independent contractor (particularly if you already have a day job), it is easy to skip that step. But, as you can see, it's dangerous. Here are the benefits of incorporating your business:

1. It will ensure the protection of your personal assets and is one of the best ways to do so. If your business generates debt, creditors can come for the assets of the business only. Founders, directors, owners and their personal assets, such as houses, cars and bank accounts, are not liable. And there's more to it than debt. What happens if you get sued as an independent contractor? It happened to me. My company was sued by a disgruntled employee. Because I was CEO, the suit caused me stress, but it would have been unimaginably worse if I had been sued as an individual.
2. It is difficult to raise money if your business is not incorporated. Most investors want some equity in your business in exchange for the money they provide. They will not invest in a sole partnership. The same is true with grants, even though they do not generally involve equity.
3. If you die, your business can continue. This may sound morbid, but it is a good thing. If you have incorporated your business and you die, your heirs can decide how to resolve matters.
4. An incorporated business looks more credible to the public, both customers and suppliers, than an unincorporated one does. It also makes it much easier to belong to a community or a society of similar businesses.

What structure should you choose? Choosing a structure for your business is like choosing the country you want to live in: you need to abide by the laws that pertain to the place you choose. Among the usual structures, your business can be a sole proprietorship, a legal partnership, a limited liability company, a corporation of the C or S type, or a non-profit. Here is a brief description of each:

1. **Sole Proprietorship:** A sole proprietorship is the simplest entity and gives you complete control of your business. In this structure, your business assets and liabilities and your personal assets and liabilities are not separate. You can be held personally liable for the debts and obligations of the business.
2. **Legal Partnership:** If your business has more than one owner, a partnership is a simple structure to consider. It can be a partnership in which all the owners have limited liability. For example, in this case, each partner is protected from debts charged to the partnership.
3. **Limited Liability Company:** In a limited liability company, owners' personal assets are protected in case of a bankruptcy or a lawsuit. Tax rates are different, but members must pay self-employment taxes.
4. **C-Corporation:** A C-corporation is a legal entity that is totally separate from its owners, officers and directors. It is a more complex structure and hence more expensive to set up, and also more demanding in terms of record-keeping and paperwork, but it also best protects your personal assets. When it comes to raising capital, corporations have an advantage because they offer stock—a big benefit that can be sold or publicly traded on the stock market.
5. **S-Corporation:** An S-corporation is a special type of corporation that allows profits, and some losses, to be passed directly to the owners' personal incomes without their being subject to corporate tax rates. There are limits on S-corporations. For example, they can't have more than 100 shareholders, and all shareholders must be U.S. citizens.
6. **Non-Profit Corporation:** Non-Profit corporations, such as charities or religious institutions, provide services or work that benefit the general public. Therefore, they are typically exempt from paying taxes. Except for that difference in tax status, they operate in the same way as a regular corporation.

How you choose the structure of your business depends on its nature and the ways you want to protect yourself. In a sole proprietorship, the owner and the business are the same legal entity, and every business transaction (revenue, debts, and the like) is the responsibility of the owner. It is a very simple structure that works well for some businesses—as long as the owner is aware of those liabilities. By contrast, a corporation is an entity totally separate from its owners, officers and directors, which makes it a more rigid structure and more complicated to manage. Because I am not a lawyer, I will not go into further detail so as not to provide erroneous information, but there are many resources on the Internet, such as LegalZoom, to help you make the right choices. It's also useful to consult people with businesses similar to yours to learn what structure they use. The next question is whether you will need to use a lawyer or not.

I have incorporated three businesses: a C-corporation, a limited liability company and an S-corporation. The C-corporation was by far the most expensive ($50,000), compared to the other two (between $1,000 and $2,500). You can incorporate a business online if it has a simple structure—only one shareholder, for example. There are resources that can get your business incorporated easily and for a reasonable fee. If your structure is more complex (say, more than one shareholder or with sophisticated bylaws), it might be wise to hire a lawyer. It will be more expensive, of course, but probably safer in the long run. It can be quite expensive to incorporate a C-corporation, but a likely reason for doing so is that you expect your business to eventually have a (positive) exit, such as acquisition or being publicly traded on the stock market. When I started my C-corporation, a colleague informed me that there was an association that helped women-owned businesses. I got in touch with it and, since we had no money at the time, after convincing them that the business offered a good product, a good business plan and the opportunity to expand, the association offered us their services in exchange for a warrant (a percentage of stock options, should the company be successful) instead of cash. One of the perks was that they used big, reputable law firms; so, after pitching our business again, we were able to secure their pro bono work and got incorporated for free—a $50,000 value! Of course, to obtain such pro bono service, you need to find a law firm that is willing to take on some risk in the hope that, when your company grows and becomes prosperous, the firm will handle all your transactions as your corporate lawyer. It is potentially a win-win situation.

Resources:
www.legalzoom.com
https://www.bizfilings.com
Your local business development centers.

OF AMERICA

CHAPTER 4

Where do I find the money?

There is more than one way to raise funds to start a business. Most people first think of finding investors or obtaining bank loans, but what I call the "organic" way—building your business one step at the time and generating sales that you reinvest in the business—is also great.

My family came from a poor background. My maternal grandmother went through World War II in an occupied zone in France, gave birth to my mom and was left to raise her by herself after my biological grandfather decided to leave her and her child to start another family. He never provided child support and erased us from his life to such a degree that, when he died in 1993, no one in my family was notified. My grandmother's only option was to find a stable government job to feed her young daughter and her own mother who was living with them and unable to work. My grandmother figured out very quickly that with only that one job, even though she was getting promoted regularly, she would never be able to move her family to the nearby city, where the schools were better, much less to buy an apartment. That was in 1950, a very hopeful post-war era. Her cousins were all doing very well financially because they had acquired a thriving "therapy with plants" business that another family member had started. My grandmother decided to ask if she and her mother could also participate, selling some of the plants that they were all picking by hand in the town where they then lived. My cousins concurred, and after a few months of success, my grandmother had made enough money to buy a two-bedroom apartment in the big city, near the good schools she wanted my mother to attend. She could have asked for a bank loan, or for a family member to buy the apartment for her, but she decided to do it on her own, which was much better for us. She owned the apartment fully and had no debt. From that point on, she built a very strong income and got out of poverty.

What happened when I started my high-tech company was very different. There was no organic growth, because I had an investor interested before I started. At first, it was perfect. Our investor pitched in by covering our expenses. Because it was my first time building a business, I didn't know how to structure things so that everybody would get a fair deal. I followed my investor's instructions and never questioned anything. When we grew, it became time to convert all the money we had from the investor into a real series of options. Stock options were a good incentive for prospective employees and motivated them to stay with the company. The deal our investor gave us was not particularly favorable to us, and the investor ended up owning a large majority of the shares. I was told that this was fair because I was bringing the technology, but they were paying for it. Somehow, my instincts told me that this was not right, so I started to bring in my company's "own" money through government funding. I also tried to add investors, but every time we were about to close a deal, it fell through because our primary investor claimed that the terms were not fair, since they had taken the initial risk. It had become an unbalanced situation, and, after 12 years of proving the technology, growing the company and building a brand and a base of loyal customers, I still had no control over the company. I felt very powerless.

I tell these two very different stories to show you how crucial it is to use the right approach to finance your project. Its success will largely depend on this decision.

Here are different strategies for building your business and funding it in its early stages:

1. Organic growth, or bootstrapping

If you have an idea that needs development, you might want to start "lean." Family and friends and/or grants are ways to get necessary starting capital. There is nothing wrong with starting your business in your garage. If you have an idea and know what your product is and how to make it, you could begin by making a few samples, using a website to promote it and perhaps even generating pre-sales. The proceeds of pre-sales might allow you to make more of your product, until you have sold enough of it to invest in a place of business, with a storefront if needed. If you are starting a technology-based business, make as many prototypes as you can, using 3D printing, for example, to see how you might add functionality to your product. Then you can apply for a grant to help you build a real product. A good website for government grants is www.grants.gov.

2. Raising funds

If you already have a proven concept or product and you need funds to build a prototype or start production, you will need to find external funding. This approach will always entail sharing equity, for which you can use two approaches:

- Angel Investors, Venture Capitalists
- Bank Loans

What is the difference between an angel investor and a venture capitalist? Angel investors often invest their own money, whereas venture capitalists typically invest money they raise from large corporations or institutions. When you are just starting your business, it is more likely that you will talk to an angel investor than to a big venture capital firm. Most angel investors will be interested in your product or technology and might give you more equity for the money they invest as well as more time to generate a return. Angel investors typically will invest much less in a new business than a venture capital firm will. A few times we were turned down by big venture capital firms because we asked for too little money to get their interest. Many entrepreneurs raise money from angel investors first, in order to start and grow their business, and pitch it to a venture fund at a later stage. A venture capitalist will expect a higher percentage than an angel investor would, which is why it is wise to wait before calling on a venture fund, so that the technology and business have greater weight to balance the amount of money raised. Once the product is finished and the business is growing, the valuation of the company goes up, which is good in a venture fund deal.

When deciding whether you want an angel investor or a venture capitalist to invest in your business, another thing to consider is the role that you expect them to play. If you are looking for someone who will give advice and help with accountants, lawyers, advertisement and the like, consider an angel investor. On the other hand, if you want someone "hands off" who sits on your board of directors, a venture capitalist may be more appropriate. Once you have decided which to choose, do some research to learn what firms invest in your industry. Talking to a firm whose expertise is not in line with what you want to do is a waste of time.

Finally, if you don't want to deal with investors and share equity in your business, you can apply for a bank loan. You can negotiate the terms and rates and decide if it is a good option for your business.

Regardless of the source from which you consider raising money, you need to prepare your approach. You will need a pitch. It does not have to be a long one, but it needs to be convincing. The pitch must include your vision, what your business is about, what your products are, what the markets look like and who your competition is. Investors will also want to see your financial projections and want to meet your team. Finally, you will have to show

how you are going to use the money they invest. Keep your pitch brief, clear and to the point, and be prepared to answer questions.

One thing I learned after making a few pitches—and that very few other people mention—is that in order to capture investors' interest, you need to tell them why they should invest in you and what is in it for them. It doesn't matter how brilliant your business idea is; if investors can't see how they benefit by joining you on your journey, they will never give you any money. As Dale Carnegie said, "You can make more friends in two months by becoming interested in other people than you can in two years by trying to get other people interested in you."

One disheartening aspect of fundraising is that you will very likely have to deal with rejection a few—or perhaps many—times. This is when well-meaning friends and peers will tell you that after a certain number of negative responses, it would be wise to stop and do something else. I have even been told, "If you insist, people will get turned off before you even pitch because they will be under the impression that you have been shopped already." My advice is: DO NOT STOP, AND DO NOT LISTEN TO ANYONE WHO TELLS YOU TO. Jack Canfield, the famous co-author of the *Chicken Soup for the Soul* series, explains it very clearly. His first book was rejected 144 times before it was finally published! When your proposal is rejected, it is more likely that you haven't found the right investor yet and you need to move on to the next one.

Resources:
For bootstrapping:
https://richtopia.com/effective-leadership/10-successful-companies-started-bootstrapping-case-studies
For fundraising:
https://www.fundable.com/learn/resources/guides/investor
For grant applications:
www.grants.gov

OYSTER

CHAPTER 5

Location, location, location

What did I learn?

"We think your product is great and we would love to come visit and work with you, but we can't locate you on the map." When I was told this a few years ago, it prompted me to move my business to a less remote location. When I started my high-tech company 12 years ago, we naturally decided that a Silicon Valley location was best. It would have been fine, except that I did not live very close, and traveling by plane every week while nursing my newborn son quickly became very difficult. So my company decided to move to the remote Northern California location where I lived. Both my business and my baby needed my attention, and it was the best option at the time. At the beginning, and for the company's first few years, it worked perfectly. We were in the product-development phase, so our customers were only "potential." We had been able to attract young people from the local community college to work for us, and the technical consultants I needed for specific tasks were always happy to make the trip to work with us.

The company, which was developing new laser technologies, was very unusual for the area, so we got a lot of attention! Being in a rural location and bringing something very different to the community (not the least attractive jobs for young people) was a key differentiator. We were one of the star businesses in the area. We were given hiring incentives, were invited to give talks at the local universities, were featured on the local news (TV and newspaper) and even had the honor of the visit of the local congressman. Another perk of being located in a remote location was that we got some priority as a HUBZone when we applied for government grants, which was very helpful for our startup. All this helped us gain credibility and visibility in our community.

After the product-development phase was finished, we started selling, and our business grew. As our business grew, so did our customer base, which now included not only people we had known during the development phase but new clients as well. We started getting a recurring question: "So where are you located?" After we answered, we would get a second question: "How can we get there to pay you a visit?" Things started to get more complicated, even with our government contracts. We were not accessible to our customers and that was becoming a problem. Another issue was hiring. As we were growing, we needed to attract more specific talents (beyond our consultants), and very few candidates were willing to relocate to the countryside.

Unless you can operate your business from your home, it is important to choose its location carefully. A service/software business can bear the costs of a big city location, while a manufacturing/production business is better served by a less expensive location that allows for larger buildings. In any case, several criteria have to be considered.

1. **First of all, choose a location and a space that you like.** Since you are the one who will be spending the most time at your place of business, it has to feel right to you. Your business needs to be in a location that is safe and where you

will have no problem going, even after hours. The cost is obviously very important. Many businesses close because they become unable to pay the rent. Your business location will also affect your tax base. Utility rates vary from state to state. You can always factor your costs into your sale prices, understanding that your products will be more expensive if you decide on a more prestigious and costly location.

2. **When you find a location that fits your needs, assess whether it fits other people's needs as well.** These other people include employees, customers, investors and potential strategic partners. The cost of your location is also an important factor. It might be more difficult to get customers or even employees if parking is expensive, for example. Customers will often consider convenience. If your business is not easy to find, they might look elsewhere. The nature of the business drives the choice of the location. If it is a high-end fashion business, it is better to be in a prestigious location if you can afford it. As vain as this may sound, people do buy status. If your business is online, you can get an address at one of those premium locations (we sometimes use a UPS store or Postal Annex address for our businesses). Perception matters.
3. **Most investors will pay close attention to your location.** They often see it as a key part of their investment, and a location that does not suit them will most likely deter them from entering into a deal with you. In the case of an acquisition, it is also possible that a potential buyer might decide to move forward with a deal because the location of your business fits their growth strategy.
4. **Similarly, the location of your business may be key in establishing strategic partnerships.** Although I am not talking about global partnerships, which I will address in a later chapter, a strategic partner can be a business that has complementary technology. In this case, it is convenient to have them nearby. Competition is also an important factor.

Proximity or distance from your competitors is a highly important strategic decision. If your product is very well differentiated from your competitors' offerings, you may benefit from being close to your competitors, since they most likely already are in a location with a ripe and established market. On the other hand, if you sell a product that is similar to your competitors', it is best to distance yourself from them and choose a different location.

5. **Does the location have a good pool of potential employees for your business?** Moving to a remote location was not the best thing for my high-tech business to do. It was difficult to get employees who had sufficient academic training to handle the many challenges of our technology—and who were willing to move to a location that presented few high-tech business options other than us. When we moved closer to a major city, that problem was solved.
6. **Finally, look ahead to forecast the future and the growth you envision for your business.** You must take into account both the location and the facility. How fast will your business grow? How much would you like it to grow? Will you need additional buildings for manufacturing? Answering those questions will not only tell you where to go, but also what terms you can accept for your lease. If you consider a three-year lease, it is good to be sure that your business won't outgrow the facility within one year. It is difficult enough to move a business without adding the possibility of having to find another renter willing to take over the lease.

John M. Ford said, "We are not lost, we are locationally challenged." Being locationally challenged is the last thing you want for your business. Positioning is a very important factor for any business, and, since perception is everything, your company's address will have a major impact on its success. My business moved twice in 12 years, and each move was triggered by its needs and growth potential. Even a great business will not be successful in a bad location, so it is important to pay close attention to where you site your business.

Resources:

If you are flexible and need to find the best state in which to start your business:
https://www.seekcapital.com/blog/best-states-to-start-business/

To find a business facility:
contact a local business real estate agent, or go to the local Chamber of Commerce.

EMPLOYMENT
OPPORTUNITIES
AVAILABLE
Please inquire within

CHAPTER 6

You are who your team is

"How could I have known that this person wasn't honest?" We have all heard stories about partnerships that ended badly. Unless you decide to start your business on your own, which is not always easy, it is very important that you choose your business partner(s) wisely. The task can be daunting, since partners are human beings, too, and even a long-term best friend may lack a business personality compatible with yours. In general, partners need to have skills, personalities and values that complement each other. Differences are great and necessary for good balance. Hiring your twin as your business partner is a bad idea because it limits creativity. On the other hand, hiring someone with completely conflicting views may cause management problems. Although there is no one matrix or equation to find the "perfect" business partner, there are criteria that you might want to consider, and questions to ask yourself when you are considering a potential partner.

- **Does that person share your vision for your business?** You might not need to be on the same page all the time, but you need to be reading the same book. If not, you will try to steer your business in different directions, which will lead nowhere. A great historical example of a successful partnership is Ronald and Nancy Reagan. Their common vision allowed them to take the political landscape by storm in the 1970s and through to the Presidency in 1980. Only in the rarest cases can one person with a specific talent do it all and build an empire. Almost all of us need someone, a partner, to accompany us in our venture. It is absolutely vital to have someone who embraces your vision and also can act as a trusted sounding board.

- **Does that person stimulate you and your creativity?** Think of the dynamic, mutually reinforcing creative partnership Paul McCartney and John Lennon had in The Beatles. They each composed beautiful songs in response to the creative outpourings of the other. Their partnership, based on friendly competition, led to their colossal international success.
- Is your potential business partner someone who can also be your collaborator? Ideally, you will choose someone whose skills and abilities complement yours, the way Steve Jobs' and Steve Wosniak's collaboration famously did. Their success was due in large part to the fact that Wosniak was a technical genius who invented computers and their components, and Jobs was a marketing genius who anticipated what the public wanted before it even knew it wanted it. Jobs would have an idea, and Wosniak would devise the technology to make it happen. Their strong alliance yielded a phenomenal venture.

These are examples to consider when starting a business with someone. However, we are all humans, and, as the Roman philosopher Seneca once said, "Errare humanum est," or "Error is human." Don't blame yourself if a person that you thought would be a perfect partner turns out to be less than a great match. As a manager, I have hired my fair share of "great candidates" who, within weeks, turned out to be poor matches. Both employers and prospective candidates put their best foot forward in an interview and tend to say what they think the interviewer wants to hear. It is my experience that, no matter how detailed and thorough the hiring process is, it is almost impossible to judge both personality and character in the span of a few interviews. Because there is no hard science or metrics for hiring, we mostly hire a business partner or employee and hope for the best. Ideally, partners sharing the same goals establish a solid company culture that will lead growth in the same direction. However, accidents happen, and sometimes people are not honest about their real motivations, so a business partner who seemed like a good fit with your vision may eventually evolve in a different direction.

After you are confident that you have picked the right business partner, it is time to think of hiring a team. Hiring can be difficult for a new business. However, there are ways to find good employees with minimum financial downside. When I started my company, the local Smart Business Center had a program promoting employment in the area and provided us with employees to train for six months, with all wages paid. It was an amazing opportunity for us to train people while their trial periods were paid for! It gave our company a big boost at a time when it was still fragile. A few years later, our company benefited from another helpful program. The city we were in offered to pay for internships for young people in high school to work for a company during the summer. It was a great opportunity for us to get some work done that we otherwise would have had to postpone while also giving back to the community by showing young people a professional environment. Hiring interns is another way to get a specific set of skills for a short period of time. Do you need a website? Ask the local community college if it has students in a website design program who would intern for the summer. You can pay them a stipend, and they get hands-on experience and some credit toward their degree. This approach saved us a great deal of money and helped us progress in several areas. Later, when your business becomes more profitable, you might decide to hire one of your interns. It is a win-win for everyone.

Again, retaining the right business partner can be a difficult task, and hiring the rest of your team should be given a lot of attention. Confucius said, "If you are the smartest person in the room, you are in the wrong room." Steve Jobs was a strong advocate of hiring an "A" team. Always try to hire people that bring skills that you don't have (in other words, people who are smarter than you in certain areas). The object should be to gather a team of people, each of whom is the best at what they do. If you need help in a specific area for a limited time, consider consulting a temp agency. That could save valuable time. Similarly, if the temps are a good fit, you can hire them full-time.

For some businesses, it is better to outsource some services. We outsourced payroll, accounting and website maintenance, since none of us was an expert in those areas. Of course, if you have the know-how, you can perform those services yourself. But if you search human resources on the Internet, you will find several platforms that handle payroll, benefits and the like. Many such platforms will also help with background checks on the new employees. They may also have people to advise you in difficult issues such as laying an employee off.

Hiring the right team is a crucial step in your venture. A team defines a company. If you are raising funds, many investors will invest in the team before the product. It is often a game of trial and error, and your team will likely evolve as your business grows. Building a team takes time and is a step-by-step process. Henry Ford said, "Coming together is a beginning, staying together is progress and working together is success."

Resources:
Economic Development Centers
Temporary and Employment Agencies
Job posting sites: Monster.com, LinkedIn, Simply Hired, Indeed.com
College alumni associations

CHAPTER 7

Are the days of word of mouth over?

My great-great-grandfather was born in rural France in 1868. He had to work when he was 10 years old to help support his family of 10 people; predictably, going to school became a luxury. He educated himself by reading all the books he could find, and when he reached the dusk of his life, he wrote his memoir, which made it possible for me to share part of his story here. He lived in a small town in Burgundy and was initially a winemaker. After a few years, he decided that winemaking was not only hard but also very unpredictable, so not a suitably stable source of income for his growing family. He sold his vineyards and invested the proceeds in a bar and restaurant located at the center of the town. He was a very smart man. He realized very quickly that his bar and restaurant could be more than just a place for people to come to eat and drink. He wanted his institution to become a place where people could find comfort, joy and an escape from everyday life. He achieved his goal, and at first it was townspeople who came to enjoy food and drinks and laugh, read and even dance together. The atmosphere of the restaurant was always joyful and light, and

URBERRY
BOS

people came repeatedly to "have a good time." Because the restaurant made people happy, they started to spread the word. Soon enough, the reputation of his establishment extended beyond the borders of the town, and my great-great-grandfather's business grew enormously. Within a year, people from all over the county came to his place, and he achieved his goal of building a business that could sustain his family.

Those were the days when word of mouth was the only way to advertise a business. This is no longer true; we have at our disposal many other means to promote our products or services. That said, word of mouth, or customer reviews, remains an important component of success because it constitutes a genuine third-party endorsement.

What steps can you take to advertise businesses efficiently? In today's digital age, having a website is indispensable. Very few businesses have credibility without an online presence. Once again, perception is key, and there is no point to being in stealth mode. Your business website should accomplish two things: inform people how to find it easily, and, once they have found it, entice them to stay on the site, to keep reading and exploring. It needs to be concise and easy to navigate. Again, ask yourself what sets your business apart from the competition and the reasons people would visit your site. In addition to an attractive business name, it is good to have a hook. For example, you might name your coffee shop "The Joyful Bean," for which a hook could be: "a place where people get a cup of coffee with a good dose of happiness." The contents of your site should be clear, simple and engaging to potential customers. The website should tell a compelling story that captivates people and contains a wealth of information and resources to help them. That information should be focused and updated regularly. In general, people enjoy visuals and respond to colors, so use images and videos on your website if you can. A professionally made website may be expensive, but there are many ways to make one yourself. There are many resources on the Internet (YouTube tutorials, Google, books and the like) that can guide you through building your own website. If you have an online business, there are also shopping cart options for your site. Then, as you start generating revenue, you can hire someone to improve and maintain your website.

Once it is live, begin establishing a strong online presence. That might sound obvious, but there is no use having the greatest product in the world if nobody knows about it. To get traffic to your website, use search engine optimization (SEO), so people who type certain keywords in their search engine are directed to it. Google can teach you how to do that. To review, the steps are the following:

- Secure a domain name based on your business name. If the domain name is already taken, you can add "the" or "shop" or a similar word to it to make it unique. For example, if you choose to call your business "Beautiful Flowers," but that domain name is taken, you can change your domain name to "My Beautiful Flowers" or "Your Beautiful Flowers." Be creative; make a name that is unique to you.
- Then obtain and secure a URL, or a web address. The URL of my website is www.freeandrichbeyondwealthy.com. When you have a URL, go as broad as possible with it. GoDaddy, for example, is easy to use and inexpensive. If needed, you can also secure .com, .net, .us and other extensions.
- Build your website.
- Advertise for it.

Use social media to advertise your business. The general recommendation is to spread the word on three of your social media platforms. For example, choose Facebook, Instagram and Twitter, or Facebook, Instagram and LinkedIn, depending on your preferences. Social media pages about your business will keep your customers updated about your company to keep them engaged with it. You can also post a newsletter on your social media platforms. Make it entertaining as well as informative about your existing and new products. It is important to keep your social media active and alive.

Keep posting videos, pictures, articles, quizzes and the like. This will encourage your customers to participate and feel involved in your business.

Does social media spell the end of word of mouth publicity? No. Even with social media, genuine customers' reviews of your business and products are important. Third-party endorsements are much more powerful than tooting your own horn, even on a very attractive Facebook page. Ideally, you can have both your own promotion and customer rave reviews on your social media pages. If one of your customers is highly popular on social media and really likes your products, word might spread at the speed of light among that person's friends. Although they might be seen as outdated or old-fashioned, customer loyalty programs remain a powerful way to foster returning customers. Who wouldn't want their 11th cup of coffee free after buying 10 from their local coffee shop? People might well bring their friends to get coffee there so that they could reach that 11th cup more quickly. When you give customers a loyalty card, ask them for their email addresses, so you can start building an email list and send them relevant information about your business, which is a very powerful way to stay in touch. The beautiful thing about word of mouth advertisement is that it doesn't cost a dime.

I have been convinced that it's not enough to advertise online; you also have to show up. No phone call or even teleconference is as effective as face-to-face contact. Choose relevant conferences to attend. Some conferences will be gatherings of people in your industry, but it is also a good idea to go to conferences that gather the people who are your customers. For example, if you own a flower business, it might be smart to attend a florists' convention to meet your peers and then go to wedding conventions or party-planner conventions as well, to meet potential customers. Several websites can help you find a list of conferences held locally or nationally. To find a conference in your industry, go to websites such as www.allconferences.com or www.conference-service.com.

Before you go to a conference or a trade show, be sure to prepare. It is a unique opportunity to meet people from all over the country – even all over the world. Hand out business cards. It is easy to buy nice, inexpensive business cards. Some websites will help you design your own cards with your logo, and ship 500 to 1000 of them to you for a very reasonable price. You can also make flyers or brochures that describe your business and your products. They can serve as snapshots of your website.

I typically go through the directory of vendors at a trade show to pinpoint the ones I want to talk to. Some trade shows are huge and crowded, so you can waste a lot of time trying to find the people and businesses that interest you. So, do your homework before you arrive. If the conference or trade show offers social hours, attend as many as you can, since people will be more relaxed and inclined to talk then. Finally, gather as much information as you can, and get as many business cards as possible. This will help you build your email list. When you return home, follow up with everyone you met to continue the relationships. Our business has gained most of our customers by going to conferences.

As John D. Rockefeller said, "Next to doing the right thing, the most important thing is to let people know you are doing the right thing." Publicity is crucial for your business and should never be put off.

Resources:
Conferences and trade shows: www.allconferences.com
Social Media: LinkedIn, Facebook, Instagram, Twitter, YouTube

CHAPTER 8

When growth happens

Have you ever bought stocks in a "small business that is bound to grow," then watched your stock (and potential money) grow quickly and then drop to zero overnight because that "fast-growing" business declared bankruptcy? I have, and I learned a valuable lesson about the dangers of growing a business quickly and recklessly from those experiences. A few years ago, I was following a company in my industry because I knew that they were about to sign a promising deal with a much bigger company. Because they were publicly traded, I decided to invest some money and see what happened. My initial investment was not particularly big, but it only took a few months for it to double and then triple. I cashed out some of the stock but decided that, since I had already exceeded my goals, I would keep some money invested in the business. I continued to follow it and its stock price. The price kept climbing as the company became a fast-growing phenomenon—until one fateful morning. I woke up, looked up the stock value and, when I saw $0, thought there had been a server glitch! But the company had filed for bankruptcy! My point is that there is a great deal

to investigate about how what seemed like potentially tremendous growth for the company turned out to be a debacle, ending in bankruptcy.

When your business starts to be successful, there is always a possibility that a customer will make a large order that looks like a great opportunity. Such orders are always very tempting. If you can produce, and get the revenue that comes with delivery, your company is propelled to a far higher level. But before jumping on such a seemingly great deal, there are many things to consider carefully. There is such thing as "too good to be true," and there are mistakes to be avoided. An unusually large order will likely push you to expand, in terms of machines, facilities or people. If all of that expansion is done for one single customer, that customer should take some liability for it in case things don't go as planned. If your customer's order causes you to get a bank loan to add equipment or other resources, and then the order is withdrawn, the situation may be difficult for your business to recover from. In other words, the terms of the deal should stipulate that the customer bears some of the costs incurred in the expansion. Another common mistake with big new orders is deciding to put all your resources into it to limit the number of new hires, but at the expense of your other customers. Never neglect smaller, return customers to fulfill a big one-time purchase order. One solution is to treat the emerging big customer as a business of its own. Write a forecast for it, and decide how much of your resources will be required to deliver on it successfully. Once you know how much more you need in terms of people, equipment and space, you can make further decisions about how to proceed. Where will you find the money to execute and fulfill a big purchase order in a timely fashion? Here are some avenues to explore:

- **If your company is mature enough and is already profitable, self-fund the purchase order and reinvest your outlay in the expansion needed to deliver on the purchase order after tax profits.** This is a powerful way to achieve growth without making yourself liable to any external entity, be it a bank or an investor, and your other customer orders can continue generating revenue while you are expanding to deliver on the new order.

- **However, if you don't have the means to take such a step on your own, once you have a purchase order and you have figured out how much money you need to fulfill it, you can show an external investor why they should participate in the growth of your company.** You will need to present a revenue forecast and a carefully crafted plan that explains how the new investment will take the company to the next level. If you decide to get an external investor, hire a lawyer to help you discuss the terms of the deal. A good deal must feel fair to each party. The advantage of getting an investor is that it can also help you finance growth that doesn't come from a single big order, but from a surge in your portfolio of customers.
- **A third way to finance growth and expansion in light of a big purchase order is to ask your customer for a blanket order with an advance.** In that case, it is important that the advance not be refundable if the customer decides to cancel before the order is complete. I have seen too many people putting in long work hours without pay, only to be told that an order won't be moving forward after all.

Growth can be scary. It can make or break your business. It is important to prepare for it, even in the earliest stages of your business. Planning for growth from the beginning is a good way to mitigate its potential risks. Here are several possible growth strategies:

- **After you have your products or services in place, you can investigate obtaining more market shares.** You can do this by offering better quality at a lower price compared with that of your competitors, and by advertising your existing products or services. One extreme (and dangerous) outcome of this approach is the practice of price dumping; that is, intentionally lowering the price of a product below its actual cost to you solely to beat the competition.

- **You can also achieve growth by adding more products for a particular market segment.** For example, a packing company that sells boxes can also start selling bubble wrap and tape. As another example, a restaurant can start catering services or sell a line of frozen foods from their menu. That way, a business serves its existing customers with different products without having to explore new markets. To accomplish this successfully, hire a product-development team first.
- **A different, nearly opposite approach, is to look for new markets for your existing products or services.** This is mostly a matter of marketing, and you should hire a marketing team and invest more in advertisement. Many companies try to find different applications and marketing niches for their products or technology. For example, a high-tech company like the one I used to lead can apply their technology to different sectors, such as medical, military or industrial.
- **Finally—and this is the approach that I described with the story—you can decide to take a bigger risk and develop a new product, even one that could be foreign to your initial expertise, to address a newly-emerging market.** This is comparable to gambling all your chips all at once. The risk is high, and the rate of failure is high; but if you succeed, the return is tremendous.

Richard Branson said, "Every success story is a tale of constant adaptation, revision and change." Growth is necessary for any company, even if it is simply adapting to a changing market. Like children, companies evolve and, very much like that of a parent, it is the job of the entrepreneur to promote healthy growth. And, like a parent, you get to feel proud and excited over the growth of your business – a fantastic accomplishment!

EXIT

CHAPTER 9

Moving to Production and Manufacturing

It was a glorious morning and we were all at work, preparing for an upcoming conference. As a high-tech company, we never expected unplanned visitors, but that day the front door swung open, much to our surprise. Two women stood there. Our first reaction was to tell them that we weren't selling anything, so they most likely had the wrong address. One of us even joked that we didn't serve food, either. The two women did not look like they wanted to exchange jokes with us. They showed us their identification cards and said they were from OSHA (the Occupational Safety and Health Organization). They explained that they had been tipped off anonymously that our business practices were unsafe, and they were there to ensure we were in compliance with all the rules. I had never been part of an OSHA investigation before, but coming from a manufacturing background with the previous companies I had worked for, I was not particularly alarmed, and I was quite confident that we were up to standards and would pass. The two women told us that, depending on the complexity of our operation, they would be working around us, observing us and asking questions for about a week. Fortunately, since we had started our research and development operation, I had already insisted that we look ahead to the future and document everything and train people and new employees thoroughly so that we would be ready when operations started growing. Compliance was one of my main concerns, and I kept emphasizing that procedures had to be written and followed with no exception. Every change we made to a process was documented, and every single piece of equipment had its own training manual for employees to follow. The OSHA inspection was very detailed, and the women asked many questions. But thanks to the care we had taken early on to document everything, the inspectors were satisfied, stayed for only two days instead of a whole week—and we passed with flying colors, without having to pay any fine. One reason we navigated this ordeal successfully is that, from the very early stages of the company, we treated it as if it were already in production. Even if we were still developing the technology, we got into "production mode," which meant that we documented everything and took every step necessary to ensure a smooth transition from concept to production, even if we were far from being in production. It is much easier to establish good practices when the company is still in its infancy.

How do you move smoothly to production once your concept is established? Again, it is very important to do extensive preparation work before even considering moving into production. A few steps need to be taken to be production-ready:

- **Develop a portfolio of vendors.** Even if you have been working with specific vendors for years and have great relationships with them, it's important to find more people that provide the same goods or services, so you have a back-up plan if one of the vendors stops operation. It is also good for price negotiation, which is a crucial part of being competitive once you are in production. Establish a vendor database from the day you start your business.

- **As you are establishing a vendor database, create a customer database too.** It should include contact information and records of what the customers purchased from you. Customer behavior often shows trends and patterns, and it is a good idea to keep track of them.
- **Familiarize yourself with the legalities of your business.** You will need to acquire licenses and certifications to start your business and permits from the city and/or the state to expand.
- **Document all procedures.** It is much easier to do that when the company is still small. Then you can simply add or amend what you already have in place. Good procedures also make it easier to back-track a defective product.
- **Scale up one step at a time.** Expanding into production can be very costly, and sometimes seems impossible, but there are ways to make it more viable financially. Instead of buying new equipment, it is sometimes possible to lease it. (Many medical offices do that.) You might be able to rent additional space to increase your facility's square footage.
- **If you can't afford a full-scale production facility and can't lease equipment because it is not a customary practice in your industry, there are other options to consider.** Contract manufacturing is one of them. A contract manufacturer will help you build a prototype and develop it into small-scale production. That is a good way to generate production revenue and grow without having to commit to a new facility and/or buy new equipment.
- **Stock and inventory are critically important items to consider as you move into production.** Having a good portfolio of competent suppliers and vendors is a must. You will rely on them for fast and consistent delivery. Since most customers expect to be served in a relatively short time, it's wise to expect the same from your suppliers. Otherwise, you need to have a lot of inventory on hand, which is not always good. When you create an inventory of goods, assess which

are most in demand. To do that, you can track your customers' habits and evaluate what they most like to buy. Too much inventory could yield no sales and the death of your business.

Another way to avoid creating inventory (and if you aren't making what you sell), is to have the product shipped from a drop-shipper. This allows you to save on inventory and also on packaging. Your customers will receive products with your label, as if they had come directly from your business.

- **Whether you choose to expand on your own or use a contract manufacturer, look thoroughly into all laws and regulations that pertain to your business and maintain full compliance with them.** For example, if you are in the food industry, or if you are selling medical devices, you need to comply with US Food and Drug Administration rules. The contract manufacturer that you choose to work with should have a good understanding, not only of your technology and products, but also of the regulations that apply to your business.
- **Constant quality assessment is a crucial part of production.** Without evaluating the quality of your products once in production, there can be no improvement, and, as we all know, what doesn't improve ends up stalling. I have often heard people say, "Oh, we are on a roll!" It is dangerous to be "on a roll" if that means you think that nothing can go wrong and there is nothing more to improve. Customers are the final judges of the quality of your products, and even if they are fully satisfied at first, there is always room for improvement (with their feedback, of course).

Robin Sharma said, "Passion + production = performance." Moving to production can be terrifying, but it is also very exciting. After all, it is the essence of a business to produce. Creating value is what the game is all about. Whether you are generating high-quality products or providing result-oriented services, you are making someone's life better. Running a business for a purpose is thrilling.

CHAPTER 10

Let's dream bigger: Going global

vue

When I was a junior manager in the technology industry, we took a trip to Japan to buy some highly specialized equipment. We met with the executives of a few Japanese corporations and, lacking experience and knowledge, I made a few cultural faux pas – more than I care to recount! Japanese businesses tend to be quite hierarchical. One morning, as we entered the conference room and I was told to sit across from my Japanese counterpart, a scientist, I noticed a teapot full of hot tea on the table and some cups neatly lined up next to it. Since I was ready for a warm drink, I reached for a cup and the teapot, only to be stopped quite demonstrably by one of our Japanese hosts. As I sat back down and watched the young woman who had been called upon after my gesture was halted, my boss, who was sitting next to me, whispered to me, "It's not your job to serve tea." I was taken aback but did not say a word. Later, during the same trip, we were invited to dinner at an excellent French restaurant in Tokyo, and as I politely declined the sake we were served, I was asked what else I would like to drink. I asked for a glass of plum wine, thinking that I had mastered Japanese

NORTH
OCEAN
SOUTH
AMERICA
BRAZIL
PERU
BOLIVIA
COLOMBIA
TRINIDAD&TOBAGO
SOUTH
ATLANTIC
OCEAN

culture. I was again startled to see that my request created a commotion. It was a while before I was brought a glass of plum wine. As we left the restaurant, I asked our Japanese host why getting a glass of plum wine had been such a big problem. He explained to me that it is not proper to serve plum wine in an upscale restaurant, and since they didn't have any, and we were important people having an important dinner meeting, the restaurant manager had called his wife to bring some plum wine from their personal reserve!

I tell these stories because when you making a deal with a foreign corporation or group, it's highly likely that there will be cultural issues like the ones I've encountered. My awkwardness on that trip to Japan did not cost us the deal, but my point is that it is critical to acknowledge and respect the differences between the two parties. There may not be a deal if you can't understand each other enough to work out the terms.

But let's look at reasons you might want to develop your business internationally:

- It opens doors to new markets for your products.
- It strengthens the position of your business.
- It may enable year-round sales if your business is seasonal (for example, if you sell surfboards or skis).
- It allows you to expand your knowledge by learning how business is conducted in other countries.

There are several steps to take to successfully expand your business internationally. First (and this is very important), is to determine whether your product fits the culture and beliefs of the country you are targeting. It is not a good idea, for example, to try to market alcohol or pork in Muslim-dominant countries. Second, decide whether you enjoy dealing with the country you are targeting. It is a two-way street, and if you don't feel safe or at ease with your counterparty, it will be difficult to make deals. Finally, ensure that the other country's infrastructure is adequate for the commercialization of your products. For example, if you are selling electrically powered equipment, it is important to know that there is a sufficient supply of electricity. The same is true with water supply. Ultimately, since power comes from information, educate the other country about your product. Once people have a good understanding of what you are offering, they are far more likely to be excited about it.

In any case, it is advised that you start planning for your global expansion very early on. Make it part of your overall company business plan. It is also much easier to study one country at a time, since each one is unique and requires a different approach. A timeline for expansion should be prepared ahead of time.

Once you have targeted a country, research what the work ethics are there, how products are priced, what payment terms are customary, and the like. Conduct market research in foreign countries the same way you would in the USA. If you can, travel to the country you are planning to sell to and ask people how they feel about your product. That will also give you a taste of what their culture is like. If travel is impossible, you can also tap into the resources of the U.S. Department of Commerce.

Once you have decided the country in which you will market your product, determine how to distribute it. The most powerful way to accomplish this is to have established early on some connections and relationships in the country to which you want to export. These connections can greatly help you understand how to distribute efficiently. Finding the right distributor in a foreign country should be the result of a comprehensive study, since it is critical to choose the right partner. You will need to carefully craft a deal that is fair to both you and your distributor. The main topic of negotiation will be the distributor's commission, since it is their only form of payment. One of the main advantages of getting a distributor is that they know the culture and speak the language of the country. When you visit your customers in that country, do it with your distributor, which will make the experience much easier and more productive than traveling on your own. Your distributor can help you prepare for customer meetings and provide useful tips about how to dress and what the local customs are.

If you are negotiating during a meeting, I have always found it useful to do some research on the customer's company and their country. I also tend to follow the news in that country for a few weeks before the meeting, so I can make timely comments. Assuming that the meeting will be conducted in English is a mistake. If your distributor does not attend the meeting, by all means bring someone who can translate to avoid what could otherwise be a very awkward situation. It is sometimes easy to close the door on a deal inadvertently because your negotiation was too strong and bold. I have a painful memory of a meeting with a Japanese group in which our terms were so unacceptable to them that we had to sit in silence for two hours! Needless to say, that marked the end of that relationship. Watching how people react and keeping an open mind are important for sound relationships and for driving a deal to success. In any case, it is wrong to assume that the way you do business is the only way, and any attempt to go global must be based on an honest effort to understand each other.

Finally, if you decide to go with direct sales and not use a distributor, carefully study the rules and regulations of exportation before you begin exporting your products to a foreign country. Packaging and proper labeling are also important to keep your products from being held in customs for a long time. Here, too, the Department of Commerce can be a good resource.

Although it can be a lot of work to expand internationally, it can also generate a significant boost for your company. If done carefully, it can take your business to the next level and even help you diversify your existing products. So, if it feels right for your offerings, go for it. After all, as Shakespeare said, "The world is your oyster!"

CONCLUSION

It might feel scary, but you can do it!

vue

Nice book! Now what? You may think that starting your own business and being successful is easier said than done. About 20 years ago, someone told me how much they admired me for being a scientist and having a Ph.D. Although I was flattered, my response was, "Well, thank you, that's a nice compliment, but science is all I knew growing up. It turned out I was good at it, so I took the direct path and did what came easily to me. I don't think that I could do anything else."

When I think back to my reply today, I realize how wrong I was. I am now convinced that there is more than one skill within each of us. I am living proof of this. I progressed from being a scientist, thinking I would spend my entire career in a laboratory, to becoming an entrepreneur and a founder and CEO—and now to writing a book to help people's dreams become a reality. If I can do it, you can do it too! We are born with an equivalent set of skills. We don't necessarily develop the same ones over the course of our lives, but we are all given an equal chance to begin with. What makes us different and what makes us react and respond differently to events and life in general? I believe that it is our fears that get in the way of our accomplishments.

If you are reading this book, you are ready to take a step to better your life. I am not advising you to quit your day job and jump into your passion with both feet. My experience has shown me that it is best not to keep all my eggs in one basket, and I advocate diversity. Many people say, "But I don't really have an idea, so I just do my job." Ideas are everywhere, because we encounter problems every day. When a problem arises, our normal response is to strive to find a solution. There are many stories about people turning solutions to problems they found into businesses. Those businesses are typically successful because the solutions helped other people.

Another objection you might make is: "I don't have enough money to start a business." As I wrote earlier in this book – and especially nowadays with the Internet and the world being so accessible remotely – there is no reason to spend more than a few hundred dollars to start a business that could end up generating millions of dollars! For example, if you don't have a product or don't yet have the financial means to commercialize your own product, you can start a business online selling other people's and companies' products and generating revenue that way. It should not be complicated. The new, upcoming generation is already unconsciously thinking this way. For over a year now, my 13-year-old son has been telling me that he might become a veterinarian because he loves animals, or an oceanographer because he loves marine biology. But he quickly adds that on weekends he will be a famous YouTuber so he can make a lot of money! Of course that makes me smile, but I also appreciate that, at a young age, he is embracing the idea of having more than one source of income.

There are so many ways of generating multiple sources of income nowadays that the only problem we have is choosing which ones we want to explore. Again, you can sell other people's products online, which is called affiliate marketing, or you can create an online program about what you'd like to teach people. For example, there are many fitness programs that you can purchase online that allow people to work out at home. If teaching other people is your passion, you can also be a teacher online. With the Internet, the possibilities are limitless.

We all aspire to financial security, and most of us were brought up to believe that it typically comes with a good job and a stable career. In a way, that is a reassuring concept, but it is also a dangerous one. How many people spend their lives in jobs they hate just because they are seemingly secure? Too many people rely on their jobs. If, for one reason or another, they lose their jobs, they feel powerless and lost. Quitting your job to start doing what you love and selling your skills is not what I am advocating here. The safer approach is to start a business doing what you love and what you are gifted at in addition to your existing job. It is easy to find an extra hour in your day to work on your other career. Yes, you might have to cut back on TV time or social media surfing time, but it is worth it, isn't it? After all, wealthy or not, successful or not, we are all blessed with one thing: 24 hours in a day. It is up to us to use them as we want.

Creating multiple sources of income will make you feel powerful. You will not depend on one job to be your single source of income. If one of your sources dries up, the other sources you will have created will provide you with what you need. You will have created freedom through self-reliance, and that is a thrilling and very powerful feeling! Since there is no guarantee of complete stability, regardless of your job, it is time to go for diversity. There is no need to keep complaining about a job that does not really satisfy you. As Buckminster Fuller said, "You never change things by fighting the existing reality. To change something, build a new model that makes the old model obsolete."

You can do it—create multiple sources of income and greatly increase your financial independence. Expand your horizon, reach your full potential, grow and help others in the process. This is what becoming free and rich beyond wealthy means.

My grandmother used to tell me, “To a valiant heart, nothing is impossible!” She was right. We all can achieve greatness if we set our minds to it. So let’s embrace it, because we are worthy.

ABOUT THE AUTHOR

Dr. Gisele Maxwell is a scientist, businesswoman, business coach and author. Originally from France, where she earned a Ph.D. in Physics, she came to the United States to conduct post-doctoral research at Stanford University. After successfully holding several managerial positions in various companies, she became co-founder and CEO of her own company and held that position for 12 years. Her journey as a CEO and businessperson compelled her to share her insights to help other aspiring entrepreneurs start their own businesses. Her varied life experiences led her to write ***Free and Rich Beyond Wealthy***.

MORE THAN JUST A BOOK, BECOME PART OF A COMMUNITY!

LEVEL UP YOUR OWN BUSINESS BY INVESTING IN OUR ADVANCED COMPREHENSIVE ONLINE COURSES.

FREE OF CHARGE

Sign up for our weekly tip (www.freeandrichbeyondwealthy.com/weeklytip).

INVESTMENT

Bundle 1:

"Free And Rich Beyond Wealthy: The Conversation Series"

Sign up for "The Conversation Series" and in one quick payment, receive our podcast series of 8 videos. In this bundle, you will receive BONUS offers to join our exclusive Facebook group of like-minded entrepreneurs and business owners. PLUS, get your questions answered biweekly in our live Q&A session.

Bundle 2:

"Free And Rich Beyond Wealthy: The Complete Course"

Sign up for our comprehensive online course and meet author, coach, mentor and entrepreneur, Gisele Maxwell. You'll also have access to worksheets, templates and other resources to guide you and help kick-start your business.

Look for those resources on our website:
www.freeandrichbeyondwealthy.com

A portion of the proceeds from the sales of
Free and Rich Beyond Wealthy
will go to **HEARTS to be HEARD**
giving a voice to heart-felt creativity for those who otherwise would not be heard.

With every donation, a voice will be given to the creativity that lies within the hearts of our children living with diverse challenges.

By making this difference, children that may not have been given the opportunity to have their Heart Heard will have the freedom to create beautiful works of art and musical creations.

Donate by visiting

HeartstobeHeard.com

We thank you.

www.ingramcontent.com/pod-product-compliance
Ingram Content Group UK Ltd.
Pitfield, Milton Keynes, MK11 3LW, UK
UKHW041822200726
13854UKWH00001BA/444

9 781989 756232